Herbs About the House

PHILIPPA BACK

Herbs About the House

Illustrated by
LINDA DIGGINS

Darton, Longman and Todd

First published in 1977
by Darton, Longman and Todd Ltd
89 Lillie Road, London SW6 1UD
© 1977 Philippa Back
All illustrative material © 1977
Darton, Longman and Todd Ltd

ISBN 0 232 51389 9

Cover by Yvonne Skargon

The colour photograph in the centre of this
book is by Peter John Gates Ltd

Printed in Great Britain by
Cox & Wyman Ltd, London, Reading and Fakenham

Contents

I

Alphabetical List of Herbs

There are many herbs mentioned in the following list that can be found growing wild in the countryside. The fact that they grow wild is not a licence to pick or to remove all you need. This list will help you recognise them in their natural habitat and indicates how best you can reproduce these conditions in your own garden, ensuring sturdy healthy plants.

The following points should be remembered:

1. The conservation of wild plants is important to the countryside. Indiscriminate picking, or trampling, will cause eventual extinction.

2. Flowers, leaves and berries should only be picked when it is clear that by doing so no permanent damage will result.

3. It is essential to identify herbs picked from the wild correctly before preparing them for culinary or medicinal use.

4. Under the Conservation of Wild Creatures and Wild Plants Act 1975, it is an offence for an unauthorised person to uproot wild plants, or to pick any of the rare plants which are protected by this law.

5. Finally unknown to the picker, the wild plants may have been subjected to chemical sprays blown from neighbouring fields or, if by the roadside, to constant fumes from passing traffic. It is much safer to grow your own plants.

Note: The book Profitable Herbs *referred to in the following pages is by Philippa Back (Darton, Longman and Todd, 1977).*

ANGELICA
Angelica archangelica

A biennial growing up to 180cm (6 ft) high, angelica has thick hollow stems and large fragrant leaves. Honey-scented greenish-white flowers appear from June to August. It can be found growing wild along river banks and damp meadows, but the flavour is best when the plant is grown in the garden.

To cultivate: see *Profitable Herbs*.

Parts used: roots, leaves, leaf stalks, young stems and seeds.

Time to pick: leaves, leaf stalks and stems throughout growing season but before flowering, seeds in the autumn, gather roots in the second year.

Use leaves, fresh or dried, for flavouring fruit salads and drinks. Add leaf stalks, stems or roots to jams and jellies and when cooking tart fruits – this cuts down the amount of sugar required. Candied stems and stalks are used for cake decoration and in ice-cream.

Medicinally, angelica is good for the digestion, for coughs, colds and as a syrup for sore throats. Use externally as a compress or ointment to stop itching and soothe the skin.

BARBERRY
Berberis vulgaris

A deciduous bushy shrub, barberry grows 90–160cm (3–8 ft) high. The pale green leaves are oval shaped and the stems have sharp thorns. Small pale yellow flowers appear in June followed in August and September by clusters of bright red berries, each berry about 1¼cm (½ in) long. It can be found growing wild in hedges and copses.

To cultivate: Propagate in October by cuttings or layer young shoots from the lower branches. Plant out the following autumn. Seed sown in a sheltered spot in autumn will germinate in spring.

Parts used: the berries.

Time to pick: October. Berries must be absolutely ripe before gathering.

Use to make jelly and pickles to accompany savoury dishes. Use candied berries to decorate sweet dishes.

Medicinally a syrup of the berries makes an effective remedy for sore throats.

BASIL
Ocimum basilicum

All varieties are annuals, sweet and opal basil grow 30–60cm (1–2 ft) high, bush basil grows up to 30cm (1 ft). Sweet basil has smooth dark green leaves; the opal has purple leaves, and the bush basil leaves are small and rather pale. The flowers are white. It cannot be found growing wild.

To cultivate: see *Profitable Herbs*.

Parts used: the leaves.

Time to pick: from June onwards.

Use mainly as a seasoning herb. Add to salads, egg and tomato dishes, mushrooms, pasta sauce and vinegar.

Plants in the house act as insect repellant.

Medicinally, basil infusion is a mild laxative.

BORAGE
Borago officinalis

A hardy annual, borage grows 45cm (1½ ft) high with large coarse leaves which are rough and prickly. The star shaped flowers are bright blue. It is normally grown in the garden but it can occasionally be found as a garden escape on waste land. It re-seeds itself freely.

To cultivate: see *Profitable Herbs*.

Parts used: young leaves and flowers.

Time to pick: throughout the growing season.

Use young leaves in salads, pickles, as a cooked vegetable and to give a cucumber flavour to summer drinks.

Use the flowers in salads and, candied, for decoration.

COLTSFOOT
Tussilago farfara

A low-growing hardy perennial, coltsfoot has long creeping roots and flowers which grow up to 60cm (2 ft) high. The stalked fragrant grey-green leaves are hoof-shaped and covered on the underside with white woolly hairs. These can grow quite large in places and appear only after the flowers have died down. The round bright yellow drooping flower heads, one to each stem, bloom in February and March. A very common wild plant, it can be found in moist and dry places growing in poor, rather heavy soils.

To cultivate: sow seed in April or May in flowering position and thin to 30cm (1 ft) apart. Divide plants in autumn.

Once established it is difficult to contain and should only be grown on a patch of waste ground.

Parts used: leaves and flowers.

When to pick: flowers in March, leaves when small, in early summer.

Use fresh young leaves in fritters with egg and cheese dishes. Use the flowers to make wine.

Medicinally, an infusion of dried or fresh leaves is taken for coughs and colds. Candy or syrup made from the leaves is used for the same purpose.

DANDELION
Taraxacum officinale

A hardy perennial with the flower stems growing up to 30cm (1 ft) high. The sharply toothed leaves form flat rosettes on the ground. The fleshy hollow stem carries a single bright yellow flower. A very common plant, dandelion grows wild almost everywhere, and unless you wish to have a more succulent leafed variety, there is little need to cultivate it.

To cultivate: sow seed in April in an unused patch of garden in a shady spot. For best results do not cut until it is well established.

Parts used: leaves, roots and flowers.

Time to pick: gather leaves throughout the growing season. Dig up the roots in spring or autumn.

Use young leaves in salads, as a green vegetable and to make dandelion tea. Use the flowers for making wine and the roots as a coffee substitute.

Medicinally, the infusion helps to ease stiff joints and provides a diuretic drink.

DILL
Anethum graveolens

A hardy annual, dill grows up to 90cm (3 ft) high. Very finely divided leaves grow from a thick stem and tiny yellow flowers appear in July and August. A garden plant only – it is rarely found growing wild.

To cultivate: see *Profitable Herbs*.

Parts used: leaves and seeds.

Time to pick: leaves throughout the growing season. The seed in autumn, when brown and dry.

Use dill leaves with cucumbers, in soups, and when cooking vegetables such as beans, carrots and cabbage. Add to potato and other vegetable salads and to scrambled eggs. Use leaves and seeds when making pickles or chutneys and summer drinks.

Medicinally, the infusion is good for the digestion. Chew seeds for bad breath.

ELDER
Sambucus nigra

A large hardy bush or tree, elder can grow up to 9m (30 ft) high. Each leaf is made up of 5 leaflets, finely toothed and smooth. The creamy white flowers grow in flat-topped clusters and appear in June and July. The berries which follow are shiny black on red stalks. It can be found growing wild in hedges, woods and on waste land throughout the country.

To cultivate: propagate by dividing roots or taking cuttings from bare shoots in autumn. Plant in a moist sunny position. Prune established bushes in early spring before growth starts.

Parts used: flowers and berries.

Time to pick: flowers in June and July, berries in September and October when ripe and hanging downwards.

Use elderflowers for teas, summer drinks, wines and ices. Berries should always be used cooked for wines, sauces, jams, jellies and fruit pies. Use dried berries in place of currants in baking.

Medicinally, use elderflowers for a soothing drink and to make an ointment for chilblains and chapped hands.

GARLIC
Allium sativum

A hardy perennial of the onion family, garlic grows 30–90cm (1–3 ft) high. It has long flat narrow leaves tapering to a point. The bulb is made up of small bulblets called 'cloves' and these have a strong pungent flavour. The flowers are greenish white and grow on stalks directly from the bulb. A cultivated plant only. The true garlic is unlikely to be found growing wild.

To cultivate: see *Profitable Herbs*.

Parts used: the bulbs.

Time to pick: Dig up bulbs when leaves have died down in September.

Use dried garlic as seasoning. Use fresh cloves sparingly to bring out the flavours in all savoury dishes. Add to mushrooms, soups and salads.

Medicinally, garlic is good for the digestion.

HAWTHORN
Crataegus oxycantha

A deciduous bush or tree, hawthorn is very quick growing. Often used as a thorny hedge plant. The leaves are small and shiny and are divided roughly into three lobes. The tiny flowers, which can be white or pink, grow in clusters and appear in May or June. The 'haws' or fruits follow in the autumn and are bright red with a yellowish pulp and 2 or 3 seeds inside. It can be found growing wild in hedges and along roadsides throughout the country.

To cultivate: for hedging, plant young thorn sets from November to March in rich ordinary soil 10cm (4 in) apart for a single row and 15cm (6 in) apart for a double row. Plant trees and shrubs in woods and shrubberies. Prune in July and August.

Parts used: flowers, fruit (haws) and seeds.

Time to pick: flowers in May, 'haws' in October when fully ripe and firm, and throughout the winter for the seeds.

Use flowers for a soothing tea, in wines and summer drinks. Use 'haws' for a jelly and seeds as coffee substitute.

HONEYSUCKLE
Lonicera periclymenum

A fragrant climbing perennial shrub, honeysuckle can grow up to 6m (20 ft) high. The leaves are a thin oval shape and smooth. The creamy-white flowers are stalkless and grow in whorls of three or four trumpet shaped blossoms at the end of the branches. They appear from June to September. The fruit is a fleshy red berry. It can be found growing wild in woods and along hedgerows almost everywhere.

To cultivate: plant seeds or rooted cuttings from October to April in ordinary soil in a sunny position, preferably by a south or west wall or fence. Top dress with manure in March or April. Prune in February when shoots of previous year's growth should be cut to within 3–7cm (1–3 in) of base. Plants should be watered freely in dry weather.

Parts used: the flowers.

When to pick: June to September.

Use flowers to make syrup for sweetening fruits and puddings and for a conserve.

Use in ointment for sunburn.

HORSERADISH
Cochlearia armoracia

A very hardy perennial, horse-radish grows 60–90cm (2–3 ft) high with large oblong leaves. Small white flowers appear in July. It can be found growing wild on waste land, but it is mainly a garden plant.

To cultivate: plant young shoots in any position in spring, in well worked soil so that the roots can grow long and straight.

Parts used: the roots.

Time to pick: throughout the growing season.

For drying and preserving dig up a sufficient quantity of roots just before flowering.

Use grated horeradish as a condiment, in salad dressings, cold sauces and herb butters.

Medicinally, use externally as a poultice on insect bites or an embrocation for treating chilblains and easing aching limbs.

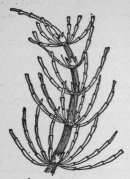

HORSETAIL
Equisetum arvense

A small herbaceous perennial, horsetail grows 20–60cm (8 in–2 ft) high. It has frond-like branches and creeping underground rhizomes. In early spring fertile cones grow on erect brown stems. Later, bright green slender jointed branches appear. It can be found growing abundantly on loam and sandy soils on waste ground.

To cultivate: sow tubers or spores in spring or autumn in a sunny position in a light loam or sandy soil. Once established the plant will quickly spread.

Parts used: green barren stems.

Time to pick: cut the stems close to the base of the plant in June and July.

Medicinally, use a strong infusion of horsetail to restore facial skin tone after illness, and for splitting nails.

Use for cleaning pewter.

LIQUORICE
Glycyrrhiza glabra

A perennial shrub, liquorice grows 60–120cm (2–4 ft) high. The smooth dark green leaves are divided into 4 or 5 pairs of leaflets. Small yellowy white or purple flowers grow in spikes and appear from June to August. The roots grow very long both downwards and sideways. They are brown and wrinkled outside and yellow inside; they have a sweet taste. Except in warm climates it is never found growing wild.

To cultivate: plant 15cm (6 in) lengths of side roots or runners in February or March. Put into well manured rich sandy soil near water but in a very sheltered sunny position. It cannot withstand frost. Plant the lengths 10–15cm (4–6 in) deep and 45cm (18 in) apart.

Parts used: the roots.

When to pick: carefully dig up roots in late autumn at the end of the third or fourth season of cultivation. Reserve the soft young shoots for propagation.

Use liquorice to sweeten tart stewed fruits and for a thirst quenching drink.

Medicinally, use the infusion as a gargle for sore throat, and for coughs and chesty colds. It is also a mild laxative. For those who suffer from acne and have a sweet tooth, liquorice sweets are the best ones to eat.

LOVAGE
Levisticum officinale

A hardy perennial, lovage grows up to 150cm (5 ft) high. The large pale green leaves are divided into leaflets. The greenish yellow flowers grow in large clusters and appear from June to August. It is a cultivated plant only. The wild species, Alexanders, is similar in appearance but with stronger more pungent flavour. It can be found on roadsides and waste land near coasts.

To cultivate: see *Profitable Herbs*.

Parts used: leaves, stems and seeds.

When to pick: leaves and stems throughout the growing season. Gather seed heads before seeds begin to fall.

Use leaves in broths, sauces and salads, and stems as a vegetable. Use seeds in fruit salad and drinks.

Medicinally, the infusion is good for the digestion and stimulates the kidneys.

MARIGOLD
Calendula officinalis

A hardy annual, marigold grows 30–60cm (1–2 ft) high. The leaves are thick and lance-shaped. The flowers, a bright orange yellow, bloom all summer long. Cannot be found growing wild but is an easy plant to grow in the garden or in a container.

To cultivate: see *Profitable Herbs.*

Parts used: flower petals and leaves.

When to pick: leaves throughout the season and petals when flowers are fully open.

Use the flower petals in broths, salads and sauces, with eggs and cheese. Add to summer drinks.

Medicinally, a lotion made with petals is for sprains and an ointment for sunburn and chapped lips or hands. An infusion of the leaves makes a soothing footbath, and a petal oil is for skin complaints.

MARJORAM
Origanum majorana

A perennial plant in warm climates, elsewhere it has to be grown as an annual. It grows about 30cm (1 ft) high with small leaves; the tiny greeny white flowers form small bunched heads, which look like knots. They flower in July. Wild marjoram (*origanum vulgare*) can be found growing on chalky soils. It is a perennial and the flowers are pale lilac.

To cultivate: see *Profitable Herbs*.

Parts used: the leaves.

Time to pick: throughout the growing season.

Use in soups, salads, sauces, with eggs and cheese and with vegetables.

Medicinally, use a warm infusion for headaches, a hot fomentation for aching limbs and oil of marjoram for toothache.

MINT

Mentha viridis (spearmint) : Mentha rotundiflora (apple or Bowles mint) : Mentha citrata (orange mint) : Mentha piperita (peppermint)

All mints are perennials with a creeping, almost galloping rootstock. They grow 30–60cm (1–2 ft) high and the flowers, which are varying shades of pink and purple, appear in late summer. Spearmint has lance shaped leaves and narrow, pointed flower spikes. Applemint has round woolly leaves. Orange mint is low-growing and has smooth dark green leaves with a purple tinge. Peppermint has very dark purplish green leaves and red stalks. Some of the mints can be found growing wild along the banks of streams and in other moist soils.

To cultivate: see *Profitable Herbs*.

Parts used: the leaves.

Time to pick: throughout the growing season.

Use leaves of all mints in drinks, wine and fruit cups, salads and sauces, with eggs and cheese, in fruit and ices. Add spearmint or Bowles mint to vegetables.

Medicinally, use the infusion as a soothing tea, rub fresh leaves on the forehead for a headache and use oil of peppermint for toothache.

Dried mint leaves help to repel moths.

MUGWORT
Artemisia vulgaris

A woody reddish stemmed perennial, mugwort grows 60–90cm (2–3 ft) high. The segmented leaves are dark green, smooth on top and covered with a white down on the underside. The leaf segments are pointed. Small oval shaped flowers of a pale yellow or reddish tinge appear from July onwards. It can be found growing wild along hedges and roadsides almost everywhere.

To cultivate: propagate by root division or cuttings taken in the spring. Plant 60cm (2 ft) apart in any soil and in any position.

Parts used: leaves and flower shoots.

Time to pick: leaves throughout the growing season, flower buds as they appear.

Use dried flower shoots as seasoning, fresh in raw vegetable salads.

Medicinally, mugwort infusion encourages the appetite. Use for sore and blistered feet.

Use as a moth repellant.

NASTURTIUM
Tropaeolum majus

A hardy climbing or trailing annual, nasturtium has smooth circular leaves. The brilliant orange trumpet shaped flowers bloom all summer long and are followed by fat seeds. It can sometimes be found growing wild but is mainly a garden plant.

To cultivate: see *Profitable Herbs*.

Parts used: flowers, leaves and seeds.

When to pick: flowers and leaves throughout summer, seeds in autumn.

Use fresh young leaves and flowers as a last minute addition to green and vegetable salads. Use dried leaves as seasoning. Pickle the seeds to use in place of capers.

Medicinally, use for colds and influenza as it has a high content of Vitamin C. Take only in moderation.

ROSEHIPS
Rosa canina (dog or wild rose)
Rosa rubiginosa (sweetbriar)

The fruit of the perennial wild rose, rosehips are bright scarlet, oval shaped and appear in autumn. The dog rose grows from 90cm–2½m (3–9 ft) high. The stems are arched and covered with curved thorns. The leaves consist of 3–5 pairs of leaflets. Fragrant pale pink or white flowers appear in June and July. The sweetbriar rose is a smaller shrub. Dog roses can be found growing wild in hedges and fields throughout the country. The sweetbriar is found on chalky soils.

To cultivate: plant bushes 90cm (3 ft) apart in any position in the autumn. Water well until established. Keep in manageable shape by pruning after hips have been gathered.

Parts used: the fruits.

When to pick: after the first frost when the hips will be slightly soft. For drying, pick when firm but fully ripe.

Use fresh or dried hips to make purée, sauces, ices and syrup.

Medicinally, rosehip tea is refreshing and slightly diuretic with a high content of Vitamin C.

ROSEMARY
Rosmarinus officinalis

A sweet-scented evergreen shrub, rosemary grows up to 1–1½m (4–5 ft) high in a sheltered position. The spiky leaves are about 2½cm (1 in) long, green on top and grey beneath. The small pale blue flowers grow in little clusters up the stems. It can be found growing wild only in warm climates.

To cultivate: see *Profitable Herbs*.

Parts used: leaves.

When to pick: throughout the year.

Use fresh or dried leaves in fruit cups, soups, eggs and vegetables, jellies and vinegars, honey.

Medicinally the leaves make a slightly diuretic tea and a stimulating wine. Use as a moth repellant.

SAGE
Salvia officinalis

An evergreen woody stemmed shrub, sage grows up to 60cm (2 ft) high. The stalked slender leaves are greyish green and rough textured. The flowers are purplish blue and appear in July. Other varieties of sage differ in colour, size of leaf and flavour. Some are purely ornamental. A variety of sage called Clary (*salvia sclarea*) can be found growing wild in dry fields and by roadsides.

To cultivate: see *Profitable Herbs*.

Parts used: leaves.

When to pick: throughout the year.

Use fresh or dried leaves in soups and sauces, with cheese and vegetables, in jellies and fruit cups.

Medicinally the infusion makes a gargle and mouth-wash. Make sage tea for sleeplessness and an oil for healing bruises.

SALAD BURNET
Sanguisorba minor

A low-growing almost prostrate perennial, salad burnet grows up to 30cm (1 ft) high. The leaves are divided into 6 or 7 pairs of leaflets. The little round flowerheads are a reddish green and appear from June onwards. It can sometimes be found growing wild in chalky soils.

To cultivate: see *Profitable Herbs*.

Parts used: the leaves.

When to pick: almost all year round, but the cucumber flavour is stronger in summer months.

Use fresh or dried in soups, salads and sauces, in summer drinks and cups, and vinegars.

SOAPWORT
Saponaria officinalis

A herbaceous perennial, soapwort grows up to 60cm (2 ft) high, with a stout stem and smooth lance shaped leaves. The stems creep along the ground and form roots at the nodules. Clusters of large pink flowers appear in August and September. The scent of the flowers becomes more pronounced in the evenings and attracts the hawk-moths. It can be found growing wild on banks and along roadsides. An easy plant to grow in the garden.

To cultivate: sow seed in April in a flowering position in a moist but sunny spot. Take rooted cuttings or divide plants in November and plant 60cm (2 ft) apart.

Parts used: leaves and roots. Time to pick: leaves throughout the summer, dig up roots in autumn.

Use a decoction of the plant in place of detergent or soap for washing delicate fabrics and for a hair shampoo.

SUMMER SAVORY
Satureia hortensis

A hardy annual, summer savory grows to 30cm (1 ft) high, with small smooth leaves on slender stems. The tiny flowers are pinky white and appear in July.

WINTER SAVORY
Satureia montana

A hardy dwarf perennial, winter savory grows 15–30cm (6–12 in) high. It has woody stems and rather tough little leaves, which have a milder taste than those of summer savory. Neither of the savories are found growing wild.

To cultivate: see *Profitable Herbs*.

Parts used: the leaves.

When to pick: summer savory throughout the growing season, winter savory throughout the year.

Use both savories fresh or dried in soups, salads and sauces, eggs and cheese, and with vegetables, especially beans of all kinds.

Medicinally, take savory tea for indigestion.

SWEET CICELY
Myrrhis odorata

A hardy perennial, sweet cicely grows from 60–90cm (2–3 ft) high. It is hollow stemmed and has large downy fernlike leaves which appear in February. The white flowers grow in clusters and start blooming in May. It can sometimes be found growing wild in shady places as a garden escape.

To cultivate: see *Profitable Herbs*.

Parts used: leaves and seeds.

When to pick: leaves throughout the growing season and seeds in late autumn.

Use fresh or dried leaves in salads and with all tart fruits; it acts as a sugar saver. Use in summer drinks. Use leaves or seeds when cooking cabbage and cauliflower.

Medicinally, the tea improves the appetite and digestion.

The leaves and seeds are used in a fragrant polish for furniture and floors.

THYME
Thymus vulgaris (garden thyme)
Thymus citriodora (lemon thyme)

A small perennial growing 15–25cm (6–10 in) high, garden thyme has woody stems, tiny leaves and pale mauve flowers which appear in June. Lemon thyme is a smaller plant but has larger leaves and a distinct lemon smell and flavour. Wild thyme (*thymus serpyllum*) can be found growing on grassy banks on rather dry, light or chalky soils.

To cultivate: see *Profitable Herbs*.

Parts used: the leaves.

When to pick: all year round.

Use fresh or dried in soups and sauces and with cheese, vegetables and in vinegars. Add lemon thyme to fruits and jellies.

Medicinally, use the infusion for sleeplessness, for chesty coughs, for bathing sore eyes and for aching limbs. Use in an ointment for spots and pimples.

Use to repel insects and to act as disinfectant.

VERBASCUM
Verbascum thapsiforme
Verbascum thapsus

A single stemmed biennial, verbascum grows 120–150cm (4–5 ft) high on a flat rosette of large woolly leaves. The bright yellow flowers grow in dense spikes at the top of the stems and appear from June to August. It grows wild almost everywhere and is an easy garden plant.

To cultivate: see *Profitable Herbs*.

Parts used: the flowers.

Time to pick: on dry days as the flowers appear.

Use fresh (immediately after picking) or dried flowers to make a medicinal infusion for coughs, colds and sleeplessness. Externally, use the oil to heal bruises and ease haemorrhoids.

WOODRUFF
Asperula odorata

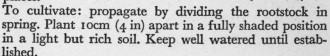

A perennial with a creeping rootstock, woodruff grows 15–25cm (6–10 in) high. The leaves grow in whorls or 'ruffs' round slender erect stems, about 6 or 7 to each stem. The tiny white starlike flowers appear in May and June. It is a fairly common wild plant growing in woods and shady places.

To cultivate: propagate by dividing the rootstock in spring. Plant 10cm (4 in) apart in a fully shaded position in a light but rich soil. Keep well watered until established.

Parts used: the leaves.

When to pick: April or May just before the flowers appear.

Use fresh, wilted, or dried leaves in summer drinks and in wines and cups made with soft fruit.

Medicinally, use to make a stimulating tea.

Herbs in the Living Room

*Borage tea • Marjoram and mint tea • Rosehip tea • Thyme
tea • Dandelion root coffee • Hawthorn seed coffee • Applemint
punch • Elderflower summer drink • Hawthorn liqueur • Herb
punch • Iced liquorice drink • May wine punch • Orange and
lemon mint drink • Red wine cup • Rosemary wine • Woodruff
wine cup • Apple juice and sage • Carrot juice • Celery juice •
Grapefruit juice • Mixed vegetable juice • Tomato juice • Herb
seasonings • single herbs • herb mixtures • herb butters •
Angelica tea • Dill seed tea • Elderflower tea • Hawthorn tea •
Sweet cicely tea • Herbs in flower arrangements*

Herbs can be used either fresh or dried in the majority of
recipes. When dried herbs are used it should be remembered that they have a more concentrated flavour, so that
the measured quantity will be stronger than that of the
fresh herb. Where a recipe demands a fresh herb which
you cannot find, it is suggested you use half the amount of
dried herb.

Dried herbs have a definite shelf life and their flavours,
scents and colours gradually deteriorate. No herb should
be kept for longer than 10–12 months.

For directions on drying herbs see *Profitable Herbs*.

The following abbreviations are used in the recipes.

T = tablespoon
D = dessertspoon
t = teaspoon

REFRESHING TEAS

Herb teas are an enjoyable way of taking something that does you good, and the suggestions which follow make a pleasant change from Indian or China tea.

To make 275ml (10 fl.oz) of tea (sufficient for two cups): Into a warmed pot put 6t fresh crushed or finely chopped herb. Pour on 275ml (10 fl.oz) boiling water. Cover and allow to stand 5–6 minutes. Strain and drink hot. Sweeten with honey or sugar if desired.

For iced tea, and a stronger flavour, add more herb. Cover the infusion and leave until cold. Chill in the refrigerator or add ice.

Borage Tea

Make in the above manner, adding the flowers as well as the leaves. It has a refreshing cucumber flavour.

Drink occasionally, hot or iced, as a stimulating tea.

Marjoram and mint tea

Follow the general directions for making teas, using 3 parts marjoram leaves to 1 part mint.

Rosehip tea

The tea is made from dried finely chopped rosehips which should be soaked overnight in just enough water to cover them. Next day simmer gently 1T rosehips in a covered pan in 675ml (25 fl.oz) water for about ½–¾ hour.

Add a pinch of lemon thyme for a delicious lemony flavour. Strain and sweeten with a little honey if desired. Drink hot or cold.

Rosemary tea

Use leaves and/or flowering tops for this stimulating tea, and follow the general directions.

Thyme tea

Use leaves of either garden or lemon thyme and follow the general directions. Add a little sage to garden thyme for extra flavour. Lemon thyme makes a very fragrant tea. Both teas are best served hot.

COFFEE SUBSTITUTES

Dandelion coffee

Dig up dandelion roots, wash and scrub them thoroughly. Spread the roots out on thick brown paper and leave to dry slowly in a warm place. This will take several days, but it is important, as it seals in the flavour. When dry put the roots, roughly chopped, on to a baking tray. Roast in the oven – 180°C (350°F), gas mark 5 – for about an hour, or until the pieces are a nice even brown. Be careful they do not become too dark. When ready, remove and grind to a fine powder. Store in a screw top jar. Use 1 or 2t in a cup of boiling water.

A delicious and refreshing drink-herb punch made with borage, spearmint and marigold petals.

Hawthorn seed coffee

Gather 'haws' on a dry day during autumn or winter. Split open the berries with a sharp knife and remove the seeds – there are 2–3 seeds in each berry. Wear rubber gloves for this job as the berries stain the skin badly. Thoroughly wash the seeds. Put on to kitchen foil and fold like a parcel. Place in a moderately hot oven – 180°C (350°F), gas mark 5 – for about 1 hour or until a deep even brown. Allow to cool, then grind and use as ordinary coffee.

HERBS IN WINE, SPIRITS AND SPARKLING DRINKS

Applemint punch

> 12 sprigs applemint or 2 large handfuls
> juice of 6 oranges
> juice of 3 lemons
> 175g (6 oz) sugar
> 550ml (20 fl.oz) cider
> 1½ litres (55 fl.oz) ginger ale

Crush the mint and pour over it the orange and lemon juices. Add the sugar and stir well. Put ice into a punch bowl and pour the mixture over it. Add the cider and ginger ale.

Elderflower summer drink

> 15–20 flower heads
> 2 large lemons
> 1kg (2–2¼ lbs) sugar
> 25g (1 oz) citric acid
> 1 litre (35 fl.oz) boiling water

Slice the lemons and put into a bowl with the sugar, citric acid and the flower heads. Pour over boiling water and cover. Leave for about 2 days. Strain through a cloth. Pour into bottles and seal. Store in a cool place. Use to flavour fruit cups, fruit salads and ices. It makes a refreshing long drink when diluted with soda water and is excellent with gin in a short drink.

Hawthorn liqueur

> brandy
> hawthorn blossom

Fill a clean dry jar three-quarters full of freshly gathered hawthorn blossom. Fill the jar to the top with brandy and cork tightly. Stand in a cool place for about 3 months or longer if the flavour is not sufficiently developed. Strain and bottle. Drink as a digestive or use for flavouring custards or fruit salads.

Herb punch

> 2 large handfuls borage
> 1 large handful spearmint
> 225ml (8 fl.oz, sugar syrup
> 3½ litres (115 fl.oz) ginger ale
> 1150ml (40 fl.oz) strong tea
> juice of 6 lemons
> juice of 2 oranges
> 225ml (8 fl.oz) pineapple juice
> bunch of fresh washed mint
> marigold petals

Pour 1¼ litres (45 fl.oz) boiling water over the mint leaves and allow to steep for 20 minutes. Strain and pour into a large bowl over the borage, fruit juices, tea and syrup. Leave overnight. Strain over ice and add ginger ale, fresh mint leaves and marigold petals.

Iced liquorice drink

Dissolve a 5cm (2 in) stick of liquorice (available at health food stores) in 425ml (15 fl.oz) boiling water. Cool and keep in the refrigerator.

To serve: half fill a glass with the liquorice drink and top up with soda water. Add a sprig of peppermint and a lump of ice for a thirst quenching drink.

May wine punch

  1 bottle dry white wine
  bunch of woodruff (wilted)
  grated rind and juice of an orange
  1T fresh chopped sweet cicely
  1D sugar
  50ml (2 fl.oz) Cointreau or other liqueur
  2 bottles soda water, 500ml each
  cherries or strawberries

Put woodruff and sweet cicely in a wide-mouthed jar. Pour on a third of the white wine. Cover the jar and leave for 6–8 hours. Dissolve sugar in a little boiling water and leave to cool. Wash fruit and place in a bowl. Add rind and juice of the orange to the wine and herbs, then strain on to the fruit together with the remaining wine, sugar syrup, liqueur and soda water. Serve well chilled.

Orange and lemon mint drink

  rind and juice of 1 orange
  rind and juice of ½ lemon
  1t fresh chopped mint leaves
  1t honey
  275ml (10 fl.oz) boiling water

Wash the fruit and peel the rinds thinly. Put rinds, honey and mint leaves in a jug. Add boiling water. Cover and leave until cold. Add orange and lemon juices. Strain and dilute with soda water to taste.

Red wine cup

> 1 bottle red wine
> 75g (3 oz) loaf sugar
> 150ml (5 fl.oz) brandy
> grated rind of 1 orange
> 3 or 4 springs lemon thyme
> handful of fresh borage leaves
> salad burnet leaves
> 2 bottles of soda water, 500ml each

Dissolve sugar in a little boiling water and leave to cool. Into a jug put the red wine, orange rind, brandy, lemon thyme and borage leaves. Sweeten to taste with the sugar syrup. Stand the jug in the refrigerator for one hour. Strain, add soda water and ice cubes and garnish with salad burnet leaves.

Rosemary wine

> 6 fresh rosemary sprigs
> ½ litre (18 fl.oz) white wine

Gather the rosemary in the morning; wash the sprigs only if absolutely necessary. Place them in a jug and pour over the wine. Cover and leave for 2–3 days. Strain the wine and chill lightly before serving.

Woodruff wine cup

> 1 bottle of light white wine
> bunch of fresh woodruff (pick and leave until wilted)
> juice of ½ an orange or lemon
> fresh fruit – peaches or wild strawberries
> soda water

Put woodruff into a bowl and add wine to cover. Infuse for about an hour. Strain and add the orange or lemon juice. Add the fresh fruit and lastly the remaining wine. Chill lightly. Just before serving, add soda water to taste.

FRUIT AND VEGETABLE JUICES

Fresh juices make an appetising and healthy start to a
meal. The ideal way of making them is to use an electric
juice extractor. A liquidiser can be used, though with
hard fruits or root vegetables a little liquid should be
added – either water or stock – to avoid too heavy a load
on the motor.

To prepare: wash fruit or vegetable and scrape or peel
where necessary. Remove stones from fruit, cut up herbs
and chop fruit or vegetable into small pieces before put-
ting through juice extractor.

Where no mechanical aid is available, fruit and vegetables can be cut up or grated by hand on to a piece of
muslin, the herbs added and the juice squeezed out by
twisting the muslin hard.

All home-made juices should be drunk as soon as possible after making as they quickly lose their colour,
flavour and health giving properties.

For quick and easy fruit and vegetable juices, buy them
in tins or bottles. Mix with the herbs and seasonings of
your choice and allow to stand for ½ hour. Serve chilled.

Apple juice and sage

Prepare enough apples to yield 275ml (10 fl.oz) juice; this
will depend on the size and texture of the apples. Add 1t
fresh chopped sage. Extract juice and sweeten to taste.

Alternatively stir the sage into a bottle of apple juice.

Carrot juice

Prepare enough carrots to yield 275ml (10 fl.oz) juice.
Add ½t each fresh chopped marjoram and salad burnet.
Season to taste and serve in glasses which have been
rubbed over with a cut clove of garlic. Makes 2 glasses.
Serve at once.

Celery juice

Prepare enough celery to yield 550ml (20 fl.oz) juice. Add
1t each fresh chopped lovage, parsley and chives. Extract
juice, season to taste and add 1t lemon juice and a little
single cream for a really smooth drink. Makes 4 glasses.

Grapefruit juice

Squeeze enough ripe grapefruit to yield 275ml (10 fl.oz)
juice, using a lemon squeezer. Add 1t lemon juice, 1t
honey and ½t each fresh chopped angelica and sweet
cicely.

Mixed vegetable juice

Prepare a sufficient number of carrots, tomatoes and spinach leaves to yield 550ml (20 fl.oz) juice – use in proportion 2 parts carrot, 2 parts tomatoes and 1 part spinach.
Add 1t sweet cicely and ½t each fresh chopped chives and
parsley. Extract juice, season to taste and serve at once.
Makes 4 glasses.

If using tinned juice, add a pinch of basil to the above
herbs. Chill and serve.

Tomato juice

 juice of ½ lemon
 salt and pepper
 1t castor sugar
 3t fresh chopped basil
 550ml (20 fl.oz) tomato juice

Mix all the ingredients together well and chill in the refrigerator for at least 1 hour before serving.

HERB SEASONINGS

Use all herb seasonings with a fair amount of caution so that they bring out the natural flavours of food rather than overpower them. The herb is dried and then ground in a mortar or minced sufficiently finely for it to be kept in a salt cellar.

The strong herbs are naturally the ones to be used singly, whilst herb mixtures can include the mild flavours. The strong herbs retain their flavour and aroma for a longer period, but even these will be of little use after a month or so. When not on the table they should be kept in a cool dark cupboard.

Single herbs to add sparingly to soups and stews, meat and fish:

basil	lovage	rosemary
dill	marjoram	summer savory
garlic	peppermint	thyme

To sweet dishes add lemon thyme, angelica and sweet cicely.

The more fragrant herbs come into their own in the mixtures. An attractive bowl of freshly gathered herbs lends an appetising smell to the table and a flavour to green salads and salad dressings.

Unless dried herbs are reconstituted in a little lemon juice they are not really suitable for salads.

Suggested herb mixtures, dried or fresh:

1. lovage – 1 part
   parsley – 2 parts
   savory – 1 part

2. dandelion – 1 part
   dill – 1 part
   borage – 2 parts

3. marigold – 1 part
   mint – 1 part
   salad burnet – 2 parts

4. rosemary – 1 part
   mugwort – 1 part
   parsley – 2 parts

Suggested sweet herb mixtures:

1. angelica – 1 part
   sweet cicely – 2 parts
   mint – 1 part

2. lemon thyme – 1 part
   honeysuckle – 1 part
   sweet cicely – 2 parts

When making your own mixtures the following points should be remembered:

1. Avoid using all strong herbs together – the conflicting flavours will spoil the end result.
2. Similarly, do not use only mild flavoured herbs.
3. If you grow your own herbs, decide which are your strong and which your mild herbs. Remember that their strength can vary at different times of the year.
4. Mix herbs together in the proportion of $\frac{1}{3}$ strong and $\frac{2}{3}$ mild. You can follow this principle throughout whether you use one, three or five herbs in the mixture.

HERB BUTTERS

A herb butter is not a seasoning in the true sense, but it is an attractive way to add relish to food at the table. Fresh or dried herbs can be used. Add herbs to butter in the proportion 2–3T fresh chopped herbs to 125g (4 oz) slightly salted butter and 1t lemon juice. Soften the butter, add the herbs and blend well together. For dried herbs use 2–3t of herb to the same quantity of butter, and add a little extra lemon juice. This gives piquancy and helps to reconstitute the herb, extracting its full flavour. Make up the herb butter several hours before required and chill in refrigerator, where it will keep for a number of days.

Flavours which are especially good are: basil, dill, crushed dill seed, crushed clove of garlic, grated horseradish root, any of the mints, rosemary, summer savory and the thymes.

You can blend your own mixture using some of the milder herbs as well, such as parsley, chives and marigold.

Use your butter directly on top of grilled meats, hot vegetables or baked potatoes. Use in sandwiches and on savoury biscuits. Best of all, use on hot bread rolls or slice a french loaf, lengthways, spread each cut side with herb butter, wrap the loaf in tin foil and bake it in a hot oven for 10 minutes.

SOOTHING TEAS

To calm the nerves and produce a feeling of relaxation these teas are mild sedatives and digestives.

Angelica tea

Make tea of leaves or stalks following general directions on p. 29. Drink the tea hot immediately after the evening meal as a mild digestive. Sweeten with honey if desired.

Dill seed tea

Pour 275ml (10 fl.oz) boiling water over 2t crushed dill seed and simmer gently for 10 minutes. Strain, reheat and take it hot for a really soothing drink last thing at night.

Elderflower tea

Use dried or fresh flower heads lightly washed. Pour 550ml (20 fl.oz) boiling water over a large handful of flowers. Cover and allow to stand for 5–10 minutes. Strain. Sweeten with honey if desired. Take hot for an effective sleep-inducing tea last thing at night.

Hawthorn tea

Pour 150ml (5 fl.oz) boiling water over 1T fresh un-
damaged flowers. Cover and steep for 5–6 minutes. Strain,
then sweeten if desired, and drink hot.

Sweet cicely tea

Follow the general directions for making teas on p. 29.
This sweet tasting tea can be made quite strong and needs
no added sugar. A good digestive drink when taken hot.

Other soothing teas are savory and peppermint.

HERBS IN FLOWER ARRANGEMENTS

Herb plants can provide material for beautiful flower arrangements, whether you like a huge display of flowers, a
small dainty posy or just a simple bouquet. Amongst the
plants there is a wide variety of textured foliage in all
shades of green and grey. There are flowers of every
colour to brighten up the vase and lend freshness to each
room.

You may arrange your flowers with infinite care or
place them haphazardly into a vase, but certainly you will
enjoy to the full the lovely scents and aromas which come
from the plants. These are always such a joy to a blind
person.

To get full benefit from your flower arrangement, the
following points are important:
1. Gather the flowers and leaves in the evening after the
sun has gone down.
2. Stems which give off a milky fluid when picked should
have their ends burnt over a candle for 10 seconds.

3. Plunge them into a sink or bucket full of cold water to come well up the stems. Leave to soak overnight.

4. If you have to shorten a stem for the arrangement, remember to burn the end again.

The following list may help you choose your material for floral arrangements:

Foliage plants

Barberry, lovage, marjoram, mints, mugwort, nasturtium, rosemary, sages, savories and the thymes.

Flowers

Angelica, basil, dill, honeysuckle, marigold, marjoram, mugwort, nasturtium, the sages, salad burnet, the savories, sweet cicely, the thymes, verbascum and woodruff.

Dried or fresh seed heads offer an unusual display:

Angelica, dill, lovage, rosehips, sweet cicely.

3

Herbs in the Kitchen

Dill summer soup • Five herb broth • Leek broth • Lovage broth • Marigold chicken broth • Marjoram bean soup • Mint soup • Sage soup • Savory soup • Thyme soup • Broad bean salad • Horseradish cole slaw • Nasturtium salad • Sweet corn salad • Winter salad • Dill herb dressing for salads • Green sauce • Herb cream sauce • Herb mayonnaise • Vinaigrette dressing • Egg dip • Egg mayonnaise • Egg mousse • Lovage soufflé • Sweet herb pancakes • Cheese and potato cakes • Cheese and tomato toast • Cheese pudding • Herb cheese • Mushrooms with cheese • Baked courgettes • Braised leeks • Carrots and dill • Creamed cabbage • Savoury lentil • Banana and orange salad • Quince creams • Raspberry charlotte • Strawberry fruit salad • Sweet apples in wine • Applemint ice-cream • Gooseberry ice-cream • Peppermint water ice • Thyme water ice

To cook with herbs is perhaps the most accepted way of using them. You automatically assume that the proper place for herbs is in the kitchen, but few realise how much they contribute to the daily diet.

Herbs greatly improve the flavour of food as well as making it more nourishing. They are full of nutritious substances, one of which, volatile oil, provides each herb with its distinctive flavour and aroma.

Meals become easier to digest, for when herbs are used in cooking their aromas are released. These act upon the olfactory nerves making the digestive juices in the mouth and stomach flow. Thus, when the food is eaten its full value is obtained by the body.

SOUPS AND BROTHS

Dill summer soup

275ml (10 fl.oz) chicken stock
275ml (10 fl.oz) tomato juice
½ cucumber, finely diced
½ crushed clove of garlic
4t dill
125ml (4 fl.oz) single cream
125ml (4 fl.oz) milk
salt and pepper

Mix together the stock, tomato juice, garlic, dill, cream, milk and seasoning. Blend well, then add the cucumber. For a really smooth soup put all the ingredients into the liquidiser and turn on to medium speed for 2 or 3 minutes. Serve well chilled. Serves 4–6.

Five herb broth

2 medium onions, chopped
800ml (30 fl.oz) vegetable stock
2T sunflower seed oil
2t each chopped lovage, mint, rosemary,
    winter savory and parsley
1T flour
salt and pepper

Heat oil in a pan. Gently sauté the herbs and onions for 2–3 minutes, then add the flour. Cook a further 2 minutes, add stock and seasoning and bring to the boil. Simmer gently for 20–25 minutes. Serves 4–5.

Leek broth

2 leeks, finely chopped
1 medium-sized potato, finely sliced
2D sunflower seed oil
1 small clove garlic, finely chopped
½t caraway seed
1t each lovage and mint, finely chopped
800ml (30 fl.oz) stock
seasoning

Heat oil over a low flame. Put in leeks and potatoes and sauté gently for a few minutes. Add garlic and stir well. Pour in the stock and add caraway seed, lovage and mint. Cover and simmer for 25 minutes or until vegetables are soft. Adjust seasoning. Serves 4.

Lovage broth

115ml (40 fl.oz) well flavoured brown stock
4T fresh or dried chopped lovage leaves
seasoning

Remove all fat from the stock and strain it into a pan. Bring to the boil and season to taste. Add the lovage and simmer gently for 10–15 minutes. Serves 6.

Marigold chicken broth

550ml (20 fl.oz) strong chicken stock
1T dried marigold petals
1D rice
salt and pepper

Wash the rice and put in a pan with other ingredients. Bring slowly to the boil and simmer gently until the rice is cooked. Adjust seasoning and serve. Serves 3.

Marjoram bean soup

> 50g (2 oz) butter beans, soaked overnight
> 2 medium onions, sliced
> 2T sunflower seed oil
> 2T fresh chopped marjoram
> 1½ litres (55 fl.oz) stock
> salt and pepper

Cook the beans in their soaking water until soft, then drain. Heat oil in a pan over low heat, add onions and cook for 2–3 minutes. Add the marjoram and cook for a further 2 minutes. Add beans, stock and seasoning, bring to the boil, simmer gently for 20–30 minutes. Pass the soup through a sieve or put into a liquidiser. Adjust seasoning, reheat and serve. Serves 6.

Mint soup

> 3 medium-sized potatoes
> 2T sunflower seed oil
> 2T fresh chopped mint
> 1½ litres (55 fl.oz) stock
> salt and pepper

Heat oil in a pan. Add the potatoes, roughly chopped, and the mint. Sauté gently for 3–5 minutes. Pour on the stock and add seasoning. Bring to the boil and simmer until the potatoes are soft – about 20 minutes. Pass the soup through a sieve or put into a liquidiser. Adjust seasoning, reheat and serve. Serves 6.

Sage soup

> 125g (4 oz) red lentils
> 1 medium onion, chopped
> 1 small clove garlic, chopped
> 2T sunflower seed oil
> 800ml (30 fl.oz) chicken stock
> 1T tomato purée
> 2T fresh chopped sage leaves
> salt and pepper

Wash, cook and drain the lentils. Heat oil in a pan, add
onion and garlic. Cook gently for 2–3 minutes. Add the
sage and cook a further 2 minutes. Add lentils, tomato
purée, stock and seasoning. Cover the pan and simmer for
20–30 minutes, stirring occasionally. Pass the soup
through a sieve or put into a liquidiser. Adjust seasoning,
reheat and serve. Serves 4–5.

Savory soup

    50g (2 oz) green split peas
    1 onion, sliced
    800ml (30 fl.oz) ham stock
    2T fresh summer savory
    pepper
    pinch of sugar

Soak the peas overnight in some of the stock. Add onion,
sugar, pepper, summer savory and the remaining stock.
Simmer gently until the peas are soft. Remove from the
heat and put through a sieve or into a liquidiser. Adjust
seasoning, reheat and serve. Serves 4.

Thyme soup

    1 onion, sliced
    2T fresh chopped thyme
    550ml (20 fl.oz) chicken stock
    1T flour
    1T sunflower seed oil
    salt and pepper

Heat oil in a pan. Sauté the onion gently and add the
thyme. Finally stir in the flour and allow to cook for a
further 2 minutes. Add the stock and seasoning, cover and
simmer gently for 20 minutes. Remove from the heat,
pass the soup through a sieve or put into a liquidiser.
Adjust seasoning, reheat and serve. Serves 3.

SALADS AND SAUCES

Broad bean salad

    450g (16 oz) young broad beans
    1 or 2 spring onions
    4T cream
    2t lemon juice
    1t each fresh chopped summer savory and
      parsley
    salt and pepper

Cook the beans until tender in boiling salted water to
which is added ½t summer savory. Drain and cool. Slice
the spring onions very thinly and add to the beans. Mix
together the cream, lemon juice, herbs and seasoning.
Pour the dressing over the beans. Serves 4.

Horseradish cole slaw

    125g (4 oz) cabbage
    1D chopped raw onion
    2t grated fresh horseradish
    1T mayonnaise
    25g (1 oz) grated carrot

Wash and chop the cabbage into fine strips. Mix with all
the other ingredients and serve. Serves 4.

Nasturtium salad

    young nasturtium leaves
    lettuce
    raw carrot
    spring onions
    a few nasturtium flowers

Using 2 lettuce leaves to every nasturtium leaf, wash them
well in salted water, shake off excess moisture and arrange

in a dish. Grate carrot on top and sprinkle finely chopped spring onions over the carrot. Garnish with 1 or 2 nasturtium flowers and serve at once.

Add your own mixture of fresh herbs at the table in an oil and lemon dressing. Or serve a cream dressing made by mixing together 3T cream, 1t lemon juice and ½t parsley.

Sweet corn salad

4T cooked sweet corn
1D each fresh chopped sweet cicely, mint
   and chives
150ml (5 fl.oz) cream, soured
1 tomato, skinned and chopped
salt and pepper
paprika

In a bowl mix together the sweet corn, tomato, herbs and seasoning. Fold the cream into the mixture. Serve on lettuce sprinkled with paprika. Serves 3.

Winter salad

25g (1 oz) raw grated beetroot
25g (1 oz) raw grated carrot
25g (1 oz) raw grated Jerusalem artichoke
75g (3 oz) raw grated brussels sprouts
2t finely chopped onion
1t fresh chopped salad burnet
½t fresh chopped marjoram
½t dried mugwort

Reconstitute the dried mugwort in a little lemon juice. Arrange the brussels sprouts on a dish. Mix the carrot, artichoke, beetroot, onion and herbs together and place on top of the sprouts. Serve with oil and lemon or mayonnaise dressing. Serves 4.

Dill herb dressing for salads

> 150ml (5 fl.oz) yoghourt
> 150ml (5 fl.oz) single cream
> ½ clove garlic, finely chopped
> 1t sugar
> 2T parsley
> 3T dill
> salt and pepper

Beat the yoghourt and cream together until smooth. Add all the other ingredients and blend well. Yield: about 275ml (10 fl.oz).

Green sauce

> 275ml (10 fl.oz) well flavoured white sauce
> 1 small onion, finely chopped
> 2T salad burnet vinegar, see p. 70
> 2T white wine
> 1t each fresh chopped parsley, lovage and
>   salad burnet
> salt and pepper

Heat the vinegar and wine in a pan and add the chopped onion. Cook until the onion is soft and the liquid reduced by half. Add the white sauce, herbs and seasoning. Bring to the boil and simmer gently for 3–4 minutes. Serve hot with egg, cheese and vegetable dishes. Yield: 275ml (10 fl.oz).

Herb cream sauce

> 150ml (5 fl.oz) soured cream
> 1t each fresh chopped parsley and chives
> ½t each fresh chopped mint and thyme
> small piece of crushed garlic
> salt and pepper

Blend all the ingredients together to make a smooth mixture.

Serve poured over beetroot salad or hot vegetables such as new potatoes, carrots and spinach. Yield: 150ml (5 fl.oz).

Herb mayonnaise

> 275ml (10 fl.oz) sunflower seed oil
> 2 egg yolks
> 1T lemon juice
> 2T mixed fresh chopped mint, chives,
>   parsley and dill

With a wooden spoon cream the egg yolks with a pinch of salt and pepper until thick. Add oil 2 or 3 drops at a time, stirring well all the time. Wedge the basin in a cold wet cloth to stop it 'creeping' and to keep it cool whilst mixing. If the mayonnaise becomes too thick before all the oil is used, add lemon juice or a few drops of hot water. Lastly add the herbs.

Leave for at least half an hour to allow the flavours to blend. Yield: about 275ml (10 fl.oz).

Vinaigrette dressing

> 50ml (2 fl.oz) herb vinegar
> 175ml (6 fl.oz) sunflower seed oil
> 1t french mustard
> 1t sugar
> a little crushed garlic (optional)
> 1t each marigold petals, borage and dill
> salt and black pepper

Mix together the vinegar, mustard, sugar, garlic and seasonings. Pour the mixture slowly into the oil, whisking all the time until thick. Lastly add the herbs and stand on one side to allow flavours to blend. Yield: about 225ml (8 fl.oz).

EGGS AND CHEESE

Egg dip

Peel some hard-boiled eggs and mash them well. Add
sunflower seed oil, a dash of Worcester sauce, a little
made mustard, and crushed garlic. Beat all together until
smooth. Stir in a mixture of herbs, dill, mint, parsley and
marigold petals. Frequent tasting is required!

Egg mayonnaise

1 egg per person
herb mayonnaise, see p. 51
cucumber
fresh chopped dill

Poach the required number of eggs. Wash and thinly slice
the cucumber, use to cover the bottom of individual scal-
lop shells. Sprinkle a little dill over the cucumber and
place a poached egg on top. Cover each with a liberal
coating of herb mayonnaise. Garnish with mint leaves.
Serve cold.

Egg mousse

4 hard-boiled eggs
150ml (5 fl.oz) mayonnaise
50ml (2 fl.oz) water
2t gelatin
pinch black pepper
½t anchovy essence
50ml (2 fl.oz) cream
2T mixed fresh chopped mint, parsley,
    thyme and chives – or your own mixture

Mash the eggs with a fork and mix with the mayonnaise.

Dissolve the gelatin in water and add the anchovy essence. Stir into the egg mixture with the herbs and seasoning. Lightly whip the cream and fold into the eggs. Turn into a mould and leave to set. Turn out on to a bed of lettuce and garnish with tomato and a pinch of basil. Serves 3–4.

Lovage soufflé

    50g (2 oz) butter
    40g (1½ oz) flour
    225ml (8 fl.oz) milk
    4 eggs, separated
    75g (3 oz) mild hard cheese, grated
    salt and pepper
    3T fresh chopped lovage
    2t fresh chopped chives
    1T breadcrumbs

Melt the butter in a pan and stir in the flour. Add milk and chives and stir until boiling. Boil until thick. Cool slightly and beat in the egg yolks one at a time. Add the cheese, seasoning and lovage and mix well. Whisk the egg whites until firm and fold them into the mixture. Pour carefully into a buttered soufflé dish and sprinkle with breadcrumbs. Bake in a fairly hot oven – 190°C (375° F), gas mark 5 – until well risen and firm to the touch. Serves 4.

Sweet herb pancakes

    75g (3 oz) flour
    pinch of salt
    1 egg
    200ml (7 fl.oz) milk
    1t each fresh chopped sweet cicely and angelica
    1T hawthorn liqueur, see p. 33
    1T melted butter

A summer spread including lovage soufflé, sweet herb pancakes, marjoram bean soup and applemint ice-cream.

Make a smooth batter with the flour, salt, egg and milk. Beat well and add melted butter, liqueur and herbs. Leave for ½ hour. Use a small frying pan and about 1T batter for each pancake. Brown them on both sides. Roll up the pancakes and serve plain with orange slices and sugar, or fill with fruit.

Cheese and potato cakes

> 125g (4 oz) grated cheese
> 2 egg yolks
> 4 cooked potatoes
> 1t each fresh chopped mint and marjoram
> salt and pepper

Mash the potatoes and mix with the cheese, herbs and seasoning. Bind the mixture with the egg yolks and shape into flat cakes. Roll each in a little flour and fry in butter or oil until golden brown. Serves 4.

Cheese and tomato toast

> 125g (4 oz) grated cheddar cheese
> 150ml (5 fl.oz) tomato purée
> 2T breadcrumbs
> ½t french mustard
> 1t fresh chopped basil
> 1t fresh chopped summer savory
> salt and pepper
> pinch of paprika

Put cheese, mustard, paprika and breadcrumbs into a pan. Mix the herbs with the tomato purée and add to the cheese mixture. Stir over a low heat until the mixture is smooth – don't let it boil. Add seasoning and serve on slices of hot toast. Serves 4.

Cheese pudding

> 25g (1 oz) butter
> 125g (4 oz) grated hard cheese
> 50g (2 oz) breadcrumbs
> 225ml (8 fl.oz) milk
> salt and pepper
> 2 eggs
> 1D fresh chopped sage

Put the butter and breadcrumbs into a basin. Boil up the milk and pour over the breadcrumbs. Add the cheese – reserving a little for the top – the yolks of eggs, sage and seasoning. Mix well. Whisk the egg whites until stiff and fold them into the mixture. Pour it into a greased pie dish, sprinkle cheese on top and bake in a fairly hot oven – 200°C (400°F), gas mark 6 – until brown. Serves 3–4.

Herb cheese

> 225g (8 oz) cheddar cheese
> 2T mixed fresh chopped thyme, summer savory,
>   parsley and lovage
> 2T double cream
> 2T sherry

Grate the cheese or mash well with a fork. Add the herbs and cream, blending well. Lastly add the sherry. Allow the cheese to blend with other flavours before serving.

Mushrooms with cheese

Wash and peel 1 or 2 large flat mushrooms per person. Remove the stalks, chop them finely and add freshly made breadcrumbs and a generous amount of mixed herbs – parsley, summer savory, tarragon and mint. Add a little crushed garlic, grated cheese and seasoning. Bind the mixture with egg and place on top of the mushrooms.

Put the mushrooms in individual dishes and cover each
with cheese sauce. Sprinkle with cheese and breadcrumbs.
Bake in a moderate oven – 180°C (350°F), gas mark 4 –
for 20–30 minutes.

VEGETABLES

Baked courgettes

>450g (16 oz) courgettes
>50g (2 oz) butter
>2t fresh chopped thyme
>salt and pepper

Wash, wipe and slice the courgettes thinly. Melt the
butter in a pan, add the courgettes, thyme and seasoning.
Cover and cook over a low heat until tender. Serves 4.

Braised leeks

Choose young, evenly sized leeks and wash them well.
Butter a shallow casserole liberally and sprinkle in 1T
mixes fresh chopped herbs – thyme, marjoram and
chives. Lay the leeks on top and add enough milk or stock
to cover the bottom of the dish. Cover and cook very
slowly until leeks are tender.

Carrots and dill

Prepare the carrots and leave them whole. Put into a buttered casserole. Pour on sufficient liquid made up of half
water and half dill vinegar, see p. 69. Add seasoning, ¼t
fresh chopped basil, ½T dill, ¼T sugar and a knob of
butter. Cover and cook in a moderate oven – 180°C
(350°F), gas mark 4 – until the carrots are tender.

Creamed cabbage

Wash a cabbage and shred it coarsely. Peel and slice one small onion. Put a little cold water in a pan with the onion, a pinch of salt and 1T fresh chopped sweet cicely. Bring to the boil and add the cabbage.

In another pan melt 25g (1 oz) butter, stir in 25g (1 oz) flour and cook gently. Add a little of the cabbage water to make a thick sauce, and season to taste. Strain the cabbage and, over a gentle heat, add the sauce, stirring well until smooth and well mixed. Serve piping hot.

Savoury lentil

    450g (16 oz) red lentils
    350g (12 oz) cooked mashed potatoes
    1 onion, finely chopped
    2t fresh chopped rosemary
    salt and pepper

Wash the lentils and put into a pan with enough water to cover. Bring to the boil and simmer gently until the lentils are soft and all the liquid taken up. Be careful not to let them burn. Mix the lentils, potatoes, onion and herb together. Season to taste. Put all into a greased pie dish and bake in a moderately hot oven – 180°C (350°F), gas mark 4 – until brown on top – about 45 minutes. Serves 4.

FRUIT AND ICES

Banana and orange salad

    3 bananas
    3 oranges
    2t fresh chopped peppermint
    125g (4 oz) loaf sugar
    150ml (5 fl.oz) water

Make up the syrup by boiling sugar, water and peppermint together for 10 minutes. Allow to cool. Prepare
fruit and put into a glass bowl. Strain cooled syrup over
the top and decorate with fresh chopped peppermint
leaves. Serves 4.

Quince creams

175g (6 oz) quince conserve
2T water
2T fresh chopped applemint
150ml (5 fl.oz) double cream
cochineal (optional)

Put conserve, water and applemint into a pan and bring
slowly to the boil, stirring often. Simmer gently for 2–3
minutes. Remove from the heat and leave covered overnight, to allow applemint to permeate. Put the mixture
into a liquidiser, then through a sieve into a bowl. Fold
in the stiffly whipped cream and add a drop or two of
cochineal to colour it a delicate shade of pink. Spoon into
individual glasses and decorate with peppermint flakes,
see p. 72.

Raspberry charlotte

450g (16 oz) raspberries
125g (4 oz) breadcrumbs
4D sugar
3T fresh chopped sweet cicely
1t fresh chopped lemon thyme

Mix the breadcrumbs, sugar and herbs together. Butter a
pie dish, cover the bottom with the breadcrumb mixture
and put a layer of fruit on top. Repeat the layers until the
dish is full, finishing with the crumbs. Dot with butter and
bake for about 30 minutes in a fairly hot oven – 200° C
(400°F), gas mark 6. Serves 3–4.

Strawberry fruit salad

450g (16 oz) strawberries
3T fresh chopped sweet cicely
1t fresh chopped angelica
75ml (3 fl.oz) single cream
75ml (3 fl.oz) yoghourt
1–2T sugar

Put the strawberries in a dish and sprinkle on the sugar.
Mix together until smooth the cream, yoghourt and
herbs. Add to the strawberries and mix well. Leave for ½
hour to allow flavours to blend. Serve chilled. Serves 3–4.

Sweet apples in wine

Peel, core and cut up apples into very thin slices. Butter a
deep dish and put in a layer of apple. Sprinkle with a
mixture of sugar, angelica stalks finely chopped, and
a pinch of lemon thyme. Repeat the layers until the dish is
full. Pour over about 150ml (5 fl.oz) white wine. Cover
well and cook in a slow oven – 140°C (275°F), gas mark
1 – for about 4 hours. Leave to cool. When cold, whip up
with a fork and pour into a glass dish. Serve chilled with
thin cream.

Applemint ice-cream

150ml (5 fl.oz) double cream
1 egg
125g (4 oz) sugar
pinch of salt
3t lemon juice
4T fresh chopped applemint
275ml (10 fl.oz) milk

With a rotary whisk beat together cream, sugar and egg
until thick. Stir in the lemon juice, mint and salt. Add the

milk and blend well. Turn mixture into a shallow container. Freeze until it is just firm – about 1 hour. Whisk the ice-cream again thoroughly. Return it to the freezer and leave for 4 hours. Serve garnished with fresh or candied mint leaves. Serves 4.

Gooseberry ice-cream

350g (12 oz) gooseberries
2T fresh chopped angelica stem
2T fresh chopped sweet cicely
2T sugar
275ml (10 fl.oz) single cream
green colouring (optional)

Top, tail and wash the gooseberries. Put into a pan with the angelica, sweet cicely and the sugar. Simmer gently until the gooseberries are very soft. Rub the fruit through a sieve and, when cold, stir in the cream. Add a few drops of green colouring to make it a delicate shade of green if desired. Freeze until firm. Decorate with candied angelica. Serves 4.

Peppermint water ice

550ml (20 fl.oz) water
225g (8 oz) sugar
juice and rind of $\frac{1}{2}$ lemon
25g (1 oz) fresh chopped peppermint leaves
1 egg white

Put the sugar, water and lemon rind into a pan and bring to the boil. Boil for 5 minutes. Remove from the heat and immediately add the peppermint leaves. Cover and leave until cold. Add the lemon juice and strain. Place in the freezer for about 1 hour. Beat egg white to a stiff froth and whisk it into the water ice. Return ice to the freezer and freeze until firm. Serves 4–6

Thyme water ice

275 (10 fl.oz) orange juice
550ml (20 fl.oz) water
rind of 2 oranges
juice and rind of 1 lemon
3T fresh chopped thyme
225g (8 oz) sugar

Put sugar, water and lemon rind into a pan and bring to
the boil. Boil for 5 minutes. Pare orange rind thinly into
a bowl and add the thyme. Pour the boiling syrup on top.
Cover and leave until cold. Add orange and lemon juice.
Strain and freeze. Serves 6–8.

4

Herbs in the Store Cupboard

*Apple jam • Greengage jam • Rhubarb jam • Rosemary honey •
Barberry jelly • Hawthorn jelly • Sage jelly • White currant &
elderflower jelly • Apple chutney • Beetroot relish • Cucumber
chutney • Green tomato chutney • Pickled nasturtium seeds •
Tomsitina • Gooseberry preserve • Herb vinegars • elderflower
vinegar • garlic vinegar • Honeysuckle conserve • Peppermint
flakes • Rosehip syrup*

Herbs about the house takes you into the store cupboard,
where herbs can provide some unusual and delightful
flavours – inexpensive and fun to try out. You can always
experiment with your own combination of herb and fruit,
or herb and vegetable, once you recognise the individual
flavours of the various herbs.

JAMS AND JELLIES

Apple jam

1¼kg (3 lbs) apples
grated rind and juice of 1 lemon
1t ground ginger
550ml (20 fl.oz) water
125g (4 oz) crystallised ginger
900g (2 lbs) sugar
3T fresh chopped sweet cicely
1T marigold petals

Wash, peel, core and cut up the apples. Put the peel and cores in muslin and hang in the pan. Put in the apples, lemon juice and rind, ground ginger and water. Cook until soft. Remove the bag of peel. Add sugar, cystallised ginger (chopped small) and sweet cicely. Stir until the sugar is dissolved. Boil quickly until setting point is reached, about 10 minutes. Five minutes before the end, add the marigold petals. Pour the jam into warmed jars and tie down the tops. Yield: 2–2½kg (4–5 lbs).

Greengage jam

900g (2 lbs) greengages
800g (1¾ lbs) sugar
juice of 1 lemon
200ml (7 fl.oz) water 3T fresh chopped thyme

Wipe the fruit, cut in half and remove the stones. Put into a pan with water, herb and lemon juice. Bring to the boil. Add sugar and stir until dissolved. Bring quickly to the boil and boil rapidly until setting point is reached, about 10 minutes. Put into warmed jars and seal. Yield: about 1¼kg (3 lbs).

Rhubarb jam

900g (2 lbs) rhubarb, cut small
675g (1½ lbs) sugar
juice of 1 lemon
15cm (6 in) stalk of angelica, chopped

Put all the ingredients together in a pan and bring slowly to the boil. Boil rapidly until setting point is reached about 10 minutes. Put into warmed jars and seal. Yield: about 1¼kg (3 lbs).

Herbs in the kitchen – some of the delicious recipes
described in this book. From left to right – quince cream,
thyme water ice, rosehip syrup, lovage broth, egg mousse,
orange and lemon mint drink

'Herb plants can provide material for beautiful
flower arrangements . . .'

Rosemary honey

> 2 large handfuls of fresh rosemary, about 50g (2 oz)
> 700ml (25 fl.oz) water
> 1D vinegar
> 450g (1 lb) sugar

Lightly wash and chop the rosemary. Put in a pan with water and bring to the boil. Boil gently for half an hour. Strain and add warmed sugar. Stir until the sugar is dissolved, then bring to the boil and add vinegar. Boil slowly until the mixture is of a clear honey consistency, about 30–45 minutes. Pot and seal. Yield: about 550ml (20 fl.oz).

Barberry jelly

Pick the berries on a dry day before they are fully ripe. Strip the fruit from the stalks, and wash. Put into a pan on a low heat and cook gently, crushing the fruit to ensure a good flow of juice. Pour into a jelly bag to drip overnight.

Cook some tart apples in cold water to cover, until they are soft. Leave to drip through a jelly bag overnight.

Allow 225ml (8 fl.oz) barberry juice to 125ml (4 fl.oz) apple juice and 350g (12 oz) sugar to each 125ml fruit juice. Bring the combined fruit juices to the boil and add the sugar. Stir until the sugar is dissolved then boil rapidly until setting point is reached, about 10 minutes. Pot and leave to cool before covering.

Hawthorn jelly

Pick 'haws' when fully ripe, on a dry day. Remove the stalks and wash. Put them in a pan with 275ml (10 fl.oz) water to every 450g (16 oz) fruit. Simmer gently until

soft, remove from the heat and mash the fruit well. Strain
through a jelly bag overnight. To each 450g(16 oz) of
fruit add 450g (16 oz) of warmed sugar. Bring to the boil
and boil rapidly until setting point is reached, about
10–15 minutes. Pot and leave to cool before sealing.

Sage jelly

Wash and cut up cooking apples and put in a pan. Cover
them with a mixture of water and white distilled vinegar,
150ml (5 fl.oz) vinegar to every 550ml (20 fl.oz) water.
Add a large bunch of washed and bruised sage leaves.
Simmer until very soft. Remove from the heat and strain
through a jelly bag overnight. To each 550ml (20 fl.oz) of
juice add 450g (16 oz) of warmed sugar. Stir the sugar
until dissolved then boil rapidly for about 10 minutes.
Just before setting point is reached add some finely
chopped sage leaves. Remove from the heat and allow to
cool for a few minutes before potting to ensure even dis-
tribution of the sage. Pot and leave to cool before sealing.

White currant and elderflower jelly

Put white currants into a pan and cover with water.
Simmer gently until soft. Remove from the heat and
strain through a jelly bag overnight. To each
550ml (20 fl.oz) of juice allow 450g (16 oz) of warmed
sugar. Dissolve the sugar in the juice and add about 10–12
heads of elderflower – tied together in a muslin bag. Bring
to the boil and boil rapidly for 10 minutes, or until setting
point is reached. Strain. Pot and leave to cool before
sealing.

CHUTNEYS, PICKLES AND RELISHES

Apple chutney

450g (16 oz) apples
450g (16 oz) stoneless dates
225g (8 oz) brown sugar
450g (16 oz) sultanas
450g (16 oz) onions
550ml (20 fl.oz) vinegar
seasoning
cayenne pepper
3T fresh chopped applemint
3T fresh chopped sweet cicely
a small piece of root ginger

Mince apples, onions, dates and sultanas. Add all the remaining ingredients, with the ginger tied in muslin, and stir together well. Cover and leave for 24 hours. Remove the ginger, put the chutney into bottles and cover.

Beetroot relish

450g (16 oz) cooked beetroot
225g (8 oz) horseradish
125g (4 oz) sugar
pinch of salt
275ml (10 fl.oz) white wine vinegar
3T fresh chopped dill

Grate the beetroot and the fresh horseradish. Add all the other ingredients and mix together thoroughly. Pot and cover. This can be used immediately.

Cucumber chutney

    1½kg (3 lbs) cucumbers
    900g (2 lbs) onion
    350g (12 oz) brown sugar
    125g (4 oz) sultanas
    225g (8 oz) crystallised ginger, chopped small
    18g (¾ oz) salt
    1 clove garlic, crushed
    pinch of cayenne
    2T dried dill
    800ml (30 fl.oz) malt vinegar

Peel and slice cucumbers and onions. Put all ingredients into a large saucepan, bring to the boil. Simmer gently until thick, about 1¼ hours. Bottle in airtight jars whilst hot. This improves with keeping.

Green tomato chutney

    900g (2 lbs) green tomatoes
    450g (16 oz) cooking apples
    350g (12 oz) brown sugar
    450g (16 oz) raisins
    2T fresh chopped chives
    3T fresh chopped basil
    ½t each salt, cayenne pepper and ginger
    425ml (15 fl.oz) vinegar
    25g (1 oz) garlic, chopped small

Chop the tomatoes and apples and put them into a pan. Add a little water and cook until soft. Dissolve the sugar in half the vinegar. Add it, with all other ingredients, to the apples and tomatoes. Cook slowly until thick, about 45 minutes to 1 hour. There should be no trace of liquid when the chutney is ready. Fill warmed jars and seal. Yield: about 1½kg (3½ lbs).

Pickled nasturtium seeds

Pick seed pods on a dry day. Shell and place the seeds in a
bowl. Cover with a salt solution, made from 25g (1 oz)
salt dissolved in 1¼ litres (40 fl.oz) water, for 2 days.
Strain. Put the seeds into jars and pour over hot distilled
vinegar. Allow to cool before covering. Leave for 6–8
weeks before using.

Tomsitina

2kg (4 lbs) red tomatoes
13g (½ oz) allspice
225g (8 oz) shallots, minced
25g salt
425ml (15 fl.oz) vinegar
25g (1 oz) mustard seed
225g (8 oz) sugar
3T fresh chopped basil
½t pepper
2D fresh chopped thyme

Peel the tomatoes. Tie the mustard seed and allspice in a
muslin bag and add to the tomatoes and minced shallots.
Boil to reduce to pulp, about ½–¾ hour. Add sugar, salt,
pepper, vinegar and the herbs. Continue to simmer until
fairly thick. Remove the muslin bag. Put into hot sterilised
jars and cover immediately.

HERB VINEGARS

An easy and pleasant way of preserving your herbs is to
make herb vinegars. By a process of infusion with a herb,
the vinegar loses its sharp acidity and becomes soft and
mellow. Consequently it has a wider variety of uses.

In the kitchen herb vinegars provide useful seasonings

in sauces and salad dressings, marinades and mayonnaise, fruit salads and preserves and in many cooked foods.

On the bathroom shelf a herb vinegar made from sage, thyme and savory can be used for bruises and sprains. Rosemary vinegar provides a hair rinse and elderflower or marigold petals provide a facial wash.

Before you begin making your herb vinegars, decide which vinegar you will use. Choose from red or white wine vinegar, malt, distilled or cider vinegar. For a sweet herb vinegar to use in fruit salads, use a cider or distilled vinegar. For a stronger herb root vinegar, such as horse-radish or onion, choose a malt or wine vinegar.

When using a combination of herbs be sure that there is not one flavour which will overpower all the others and spoil the blend.

General directions for making a herb vinegar:
1. Fresh leaves are preferable to dried, since they contain a greater amount of the essential oils which provide the flavour.
2. Gather leaves when they are at their best – just before the plants come into flower.
3. Crush or bruise the leaves and fill 1150ml (40 fl.oz) jars three quarters full.
4. Fill the jar with the vinegar of your choice.
5. Cover the jar tightly and stand it in a warm place for 1–2 weeks, shaking the bottle once a day.
6. Taste and, when desired flavour is obtained, strain through a muslin strainer.
7. Keep tightly corked.

If you prefer to use dried leaves or seeds, heat the vinegar to boiling point and then pour into the jars.

Elderflower vinegar

Heat 550ml (20 fl.oz) cider vinegar to boiling point. Fill a jar with 450g (16 oz) dried elderflowers and pour on the vinegar. Cover and leave for 10 days, shaking the bottle well once a day. Strain and seal.

Add this vinegar to a fruit salad of pears, apples, grapes and bananas.

Garlic vinegar

Crush about 5–6 cloves garlic and place in a jar. Add a
pinch of salt. Boil up 550ml (20 fl.oz) white wine vinegar
and put into jar. Leave for 2 weeks. Strain and seal.

OTHER PRESERVES

Gooseberry preserve

900g (2 lbs) green gooseberries
3 eggs
425ml (15 fl.oz) water
75g (3 oz) butter
450g (16 oz) sugar
3T fresh chopped angelica stalks

Put the water, angelica and gooseberries in a pan, bring to
the boil and simmer to a pulp. Sieve the pulp and place in
a pan or basin over boiling water. Stir in the sugar until
dissolved, then add the butter. Beat the eggs until thick
and add to the mixture. Stir until it thickens, pour into
hot jars and seal. Yield: about 900g (2 lbs).

Honeysuckle conserve

250g (16 oz) honeysuckle flowers
250g (16 oz) sugar
50ml (2 fl.oz) white wine vinegar
150ml (5 fl. oz) water

Choose fully opened flowers. Bring sugar, vinegar and
water to the boil. Put in the flowers, bring to boiling point
and simmer for 10 minutes. Strain, then re-boil the syrup
until thick. Pour into jars and seal at once.

Peppermint flakes

> 225g (8 oz) sugar
> 75ml (3 fl.oz) water
> peppermint leaves

Dissolve the sugar in the water over gentle heat and bring to the boil. Boil until syrupy, then remove from the heat and cover with a damp cloth until cold. Dip peppermint leaves in the syrup until well coated and leave to dry on a wire tray in a warm place. Use in fruit salads and to decorate other foods.

Other strongly scented leaves can be candied in a similar way. For a colourful decoration, dip bunches of cooked barberries in the syrup.

Rosehip syrup

> 900g (2 lbs) rosehips
> 450g (16 oz) sugar
> 1½ litres (55 fl.oz) boiling water

Use only ripe rosehips. Chop them coarsely and immediately put them into an enamel pan with the boiling water. Bring back to the boil, simmer gently for 15 minutes. Drain the juice through a muslin cloth. Put the juice into a clean pan and, if there is more than 800ml (30 fl.oz), boil it down to that amount. Add sugar and boil for a further 5 minutes. Pour hot syrup into warmed bottles and seal at once.

N.B. Use small bottles if possible because this syrup has a high content of Vitamin C and, once opened, will not keep for longer than 2 weeks.

5

Herbs in the Cleaning Box

Soapwort washing lather • Horsetail solution • Sweet cicely polish • Thyme solution • Moth repellants : rosemary mixture : mugwort mixture : thyme sprigs • Basil leaves • Mint sprigs • Garlic pot • Lemon thyme sprigs

Years ago there were many herbs and plants which were used for cleaning, but their preparation and application were time consuming and hard work. There is little advantage nowadays in using them, since efficient ready-made cleaners are so easily obtainable. Nevertheless there are still one or two ways to use herbs for cleaning which are of value today.

SOAP SUBSTITUTE

Soapwort washing lather

Put a bunch of soapwort leaves into cold rainwater. Bring this gradually to the boil and boil for 3–4 minutes. Remove from the heat, cover, and leave to cool. When quite cold, press through a strainer and pour into a screw-top bottle.

Use rainwater heated to hand hot temperature. Pour into a bowl and add sufficient soapwort concentrate to form a lather.

Use for washing silks, lace and other delicate fabrics. As well as getting them clean, soapwort adds a beautiful sheen and softness to the fabric.

POLISHES

Metal polish: Horsetail solution

Make up a strong solution of horsetail, using the fresh herb; for directions see p. 82. After straining, pour the solution into a bowl over the pieces to be cleaned, and leave for 5 minutes. Remove the pieces and allow them to dry thoroughly. Polish with a soft cloth or duster.

Alternatively, use a rag dipped in the solution to rub over individual pieces. Again allow to dry and polish.

This is an effective polish for pewter.

Furniture polish: Sweet cicely polish

25g (1 oz) white wax
3D turpentine
sweet cicely seed

Grate the white wax into a bowl. Add turpentine and leave to melt in the sun or a warm place. Add pounded sweet cicely seeds until sufficient fragrance has been added. Beat until smooth and pour into a wide topped jar and cover. Use on floors and furniture.

DISINFECTANT

Thyme solution

Make up a double strength solution of thyme, see directions on p. 84, and use it neat for wiping down bathroom and kitchen surfaces.

PEST REPELLANTS

Moth repellants

1. Dry leaves of rosemary, sage and mint. Mix together in equal quantities, using roughly a handful of each. Add a little dried grated lemon peel and a pinch of cinnamon. Tie or sew into small muslin bags and lay in drawers or hang in cupboards.

2. For an equally effective mixture, but not so strong, take 3 parts of dried mugwort leaves and flower shoots and add 1 part dried sweet marjoram.

3. Easiest of all, tie long sprigs of thyme together and hang in the clothes cupboard. They will gradually dry whilst keeping moths away.

Fly repellants

1. *Basil leaves*. A pot of basil set on a windowsill or table will help to reduce the number of flies in a room. Keep it well watered from the bottom so that it will throw out plenty of scent.

Dried, ground leaves left in small bowls or hung in muslin bags in the room are also effective.

2. *Mint sprigs*. Hang up large bunches of fresh mint sprigs to get rid of flies in the kitchen.

'A pot of basil set on a windowsill or table will help to reduce the number of flies in a room.'

Garlic pot for greenfly on houseplants

Put 2 cloves of garlic to grow in a 6-inch pot and place near other house plants. This discourages the attacks of greenfly on the plants.

Lemon thyme sprigs: to repel ants

Cut sprigs of lemon thyme when the smell of lemon is at its highest. Thoroughly bruise the leaves and place the sprigs around the haunts of ants to discourage them

6

Herbs on the Bathroom Shelf

Angelica syrup • Barberry syrup • Coltsfoot candy • Coltsfoot infusion • Elderflower and peppermint infusion • Honeysuckle syrup • Liquorice water • Verbascum infusion • Dandelion infusion • Horseradish embrocation • Horsetail infusion • Marigold leaf infusion • Elderflower ointment • Honeysuckle ointment • Marigold ointment • Marigold petal oil • Mugwort infusion • Marigold lotion • Sage oil • Thyme lotion • Verbascum oil • Basil infusion • Thyme and savory ointment • Mugwort lotion • Herbs for headaches • Herbs for slimming

Herbs were used as remedies long before anyone thought of building a bathroom shelf on which to put them. Herbs and plants constituted the majority of the medicines of old, and using them was the only method then known of healing disease and curing pain. These natural remedies may take effect more slowly because of their mild action, but they will do no harm and should be given a fair trial.

For best results it is important to know how to make the preparations and so use them to the greatest advantage. Unless the remedy is in the form of an ointment, oil or syrup, it will not keep for any length of time. If you need to store infusions or decorations, pour them into sterilised jars, or into bottles, and seal. Use them within one or two weeks.

It should be stressed again how essential it is that herbs picked from the wild be correctly identified before being used.

COUGHS, COLDS AND SORE THROATS

Angelica syrup

75g (3 oz) dried angelica stalks
275ml (10 fl.oz) boiling water
225g (8 oz) sugar

Pour the boiling water on to the herb. Leave to cool. Strain. Heat the infusion, stir in the sugar and, when dissolved, bring to boil. Simmer until a syrupy consistency is reached. Pot and seal.
Dose: take a teaspoonful at a time when the cough is troublesome.

Barberry syrup

Follow directions for barberry jelly, p. 65, until all the juice has dripped through the jelly bag.

Put the juice in a pan and stir in 225g (8 oz) sugar to every 275ml (10 fl.oz) juice until dissolved. Simmer gently until a syrupy consistency is reached. Pot and seal.
Dose: take a teaspoonful at a time when the cough is troublesome.

Coltsfoot candy

13g (½ oz) dried coltsfoot leaves
425ml (15 fl.oz) water
450g (16 oz) soft brown sugar

Crumble the leaves till small. Put the coltsfoot and water

in a pan and bring to the boil. Boil for 15 minutes. Strain
off the liquid and return it to the pan. Add the sugar and
boil together without stirring until a little dropped into
cold water forms a hard ball. Remove from the heat, pour
into a buttered tin and cut into small sticks when nearly
cold.
Dose: suck pieces of candy when the throat is sore.

Coltsfoot infusion

> 25g (1 oz) fresh crushed leaves
> 1 litre (35 fl.oz) boiling water.

Pour the boiling water on to the crushed leaves. Return to
the heat and boil gently until the quantity is reduced by
half.
Bottle and seal.
Dose: take a hot teacupful regularly to relieve colds and
catarrh.

Elderflower and peppermint infusion

Pour 800ml (30 fl.oz) of boiling water over a handful of
elderflowers and one of crushed peppermint leaves mixed
together. Leave to steep for 30 minutes. Strain and
sweeten with honey.
Dose: take last thing at night in bed, when suffering from
a feverish cold. To promote perspiration, drink as much
as you can as hot as you can. Stay in bed the following
day and repeat the dose.

Honeysuckle syrup

Use 13g (½ oz) honeysuckle flowers to 225ml (8 fl.oz) boiling water and follow the directions for angelica syrup on
p. 79.
Dose: take a teaspoonful at a time when the cough is
troublesome, or for a sore throat.

Liquorice water

>   25g (1 oz) liquorice roots, dried
>   450ml (16 fl.oz) water

Break liquorice root into small pieces. Bring water to the boil and pour over the liquorice. Return to the pan and simmer for 20–30 minutes. Bottle and seal.
Dose: sip cold when the cough is troublesome and to ease a chesty cold.

Verbascum infusion

Use dried or fresh flowers; about 7 flowers per teacupful – 150ml (5 fl.oz) – of boiling water. Pour boiling water on to flowers, cover and leave to steep for 6–10 minutes. Strain.
Dose: take 2–3 cups of hot infusion per day for persistent coughs, bronchitis and hoarseness. Take a cupful at night to promote sleep.

STIFF JOINTS AND ACHING LIMBS

Dandelion infusion

>   2t fresh chopped root and leaves
>   125ml (4 fl.oz) water

Put leaves, root and water in a pan. Bring to the boil. Remove from the heat, cover and steep for 15 minutes. Strain.
Dose: take ½ teacupful hot or cold twice a day for stiff joints and gout.

Horseradish embrocation

>   25g (1 oz) grated horseradish root
>   225g (8 oz) pure lard

Melt the lard in a pan. Add the grated horseradish and stir until it boils. Simmer gently for 20–30 minutes. Press the mixture through a muslin strainer and pour into small pots. Cover when cold.
Use: massage into stiff muscles after a hot bath. Rub gently on to aching and painful joints.

Horsetail infusion

>50g (2 oz) dried horsetail
>1150ml (40 fl.oz) water

Pour water on to the horsetail and leave to soak for 2 hours or longer. After soaking simmer in the same water for 15 minutes. Remove from the heat and leave to cool. Strain. Bottle and seal.
Use: as a footbath for tired and aching feet. Pour into a bowl and top up with hot water to cover the ankles. Sit on a chair, relax and soak the feet in the infusion for 10 minutes. Dry the feet well and dust with boracic powder.

Marigold leaf infusion

>50g (2 oz) fresh chopped young leaves
>1150ml (40 fl.oz) boiling water

Pour boiling water on to the leaves. Cover and leave to cool. Strain and use as required or bottle and seal.
Use: as a footbath for tired and aching feet. Follow the directions given for horsetail infusion.

SKIN COMPLAINTS

Elderflower ointment

>125g (4 oz) white petroleum jelly
>Crushed elderflowers to fill a 1¾ litre
>(40 fl.oz) jug

Slowly melt the petroleum jelly and add the crushed elderflowers, pushing them down with a wooden spoon. Bring to the boil and simmer gently for 20–25 minutes. Immediately press through a muslin strainer and pour into small pots. Cover when cold.
Use: soothes chapped hands and relieves chilblains.

Honeysuckle ointment

Follow directions as given for elderflower ointment, substituting honeysuckle flowers.
Use: smooth on to skin to relieve sunburn.

Marigold ointment

Follow directions as given for elderflower ointment, substituting crushed marigold petals.
Use: smooth on to the skin to relieve sunburn and for small cuts and abrasions.

Marigold petal oil

   50g (2 oz) crushed marigold petals
   225ml (8 fl.oz) pure olive oil

Put the herb into a glass screwtop jar and add the oil. Cover and leave in the full sun, either in a greenhouse or on a windowsill, for 4–5 weeks.

After 2 weeks strain the oil through muslin, pressing out every drop. Add a fresh lot of the herb and proceed as before. Shake the jar thoroughly once a day. Finally strain the oil through muslin into clean bottles and seal.
Use: dab on to spots and pimples and other skin eruptions.

Mugwort infusion

25g (1 oz) mugwort flower shoots
550ml (20 fl.oz) boiling water

Pour boiling water on to the mugwort and leave to steep
for 10 minutes. Strain. Bottle and seal.
Use: an effective remedy for blistered feet. Moisten cotton
wool pads in lotion and gently apply to the blisters.
Alternatively, soak the feet in the warmed lotion for 10
minutes. Dry the feet well and dust with boracic powder.

SPRAINS AND BRUISES

Marigold lotion

Pour 250ml (10 fl.oz) boiling water over 13g (½ oz) mari-
gold petals. Leave to get cold. Strain. Bottle and seal.
Use: dip pieces of lint in the lotion and lay on the sprain.
Bandage lightly to keep lint in position.
   Renew the lint as soon as it becomes dry. Continue the
treatment until the swelling goes down.

Sage oil

Follow directions as given for marigold petal oil on p. 83,
substituting crushed sage leaves.
Use: rub oil lightly on to bruises.

Thyme lotion

25g (1 oz) fresh thyme leaves
550ml (20 fl.oz) boiling water

Pour boiling water on to the leaves. Cover and leave to

steep for 10 minutes. Strain and leave to cool. Pour into bottles and seal.

Use: dip pieces of lint into the cold lotion and place on a bruise or sprain. Bandage lightly to keep the lint in position.

To ease aching limbs, make up a strong infusion and add to the bath water.

Verbascum oil

Follow directions as given for marigold petal oil on p. 83, substituting verbascum flowers. Bottle and seal. *Use:* rub lightly on to bruises. This is also an effective remedy for painful haemorrhoids.

TRAVEL SICKNESS AND NAUSEA

Basil infusion

Pour 550ml (20 fl.oz) boiling water over 25g (1 oz) chopped basil leaves. Cover and leave to steep for 5 minutes. Strain and bottle.

Dose: take a small glassful of the cold infusion just before starting on a journey.

BITES AND STINGS

Thyme and savory ointment

Follow the directions as given for elderflower ointment on p. 82, substituting half bruised thyme leaves and half savory leaves.

Use: an effective remedy for mosquito bites.

For other insect bites use a poultice of fresh grated horse-radish root. Put the horseradish between two pieces of muslin and lay on the bite. Bandage lightly and leave in place until relief is felt.

SPLITTING NAILS

Mugwort lotion

Make up a double strength infusion of mugwort flower shoots, see p. 84. Leave to cool. To 275ml (10 fl.oz) in-fusion add 25ml (1 fl.oz) glycerine.
Use: clean the hands and whilst wet soak the fingernails in the mugwort lotion for 10–15 minutes. Carry out the treatment once a day. This strengthens the nails and pre-vents flaking and splitting.

HEADACHES

To relieve the pain of a headache, drink a hot cup of any one of the following herb teas:

Elderflower: Rosemary: Peppermint: Sage: Savory: Thyme: Woodruff

Directions for making the teas are on p. 29.
A quick remedy for a headache is to press fresh picked peppermint leaves on to the forehead and temples. It is cooling and refreshing.

HERBS FOR SLIMMING

Some herbs can help the slimmer to lose weight. The retention of fluids in the body is a common cause of overweight. Dandelion, cleavers and, to a lesser extent, fennel, lovage and rosehips are all mild diuretics; they stimulate the action of the kidneys, which helps to rid the system of excess fluids.

The herb teas, or infusions, should be taken in conjunction with a calorie controlled or balanced diet if the weight loss it to be maintained.

Perhaps 'on the bathroom shelf' is not the correct place for slimming aids, but an important part of a campaign to lose weight is to take a herb tea first thing in the morning and last thing at night. The basic advice of all slimming diets is just to eat less, and one of the ways in which you will automatically cut down the food intake is to drink a herbal tea about half an hour before each meal. One of the most pleasant teas to drink is *rosehip tea.* Directions are on p. 29, but leave out the sweetening; it does contain some calories. *Dandelion tea,* on p. 29, is a particularly effective eliminating tea. Another way of using it is to express the juice from freshly gathered leaves and roots and take 2–3 tablespoons a day in the morning. Fennel seed tea is a digestive and diuretic; and chewing a few fennel seeds also helps to allay the pangs of hunger! Leaf of Sweet Cicely is useful to slimmers; used in cooking, it helps to cut down the amount of sugar required for sweetening.

Herbs do not add any calorific value to foods but they do contain nutritious substances which are important in any diet. They can also make uninteresting food much more palatable.

Finally, remember that exercise should play a major role in any slimming programme. It helps to burn up the calories and stimulates the eliminating processes.

Suppliers

In Great Britain

E. and A. Evetts, Ashfields Herb Nursery, Hinstock, Market Drayton, Shropshire

Daphne ffiske Herb Nursery, 2 Station New Road, Brundall, Norwich NR 13 5PQ

Tumblers Bottom Herb Farm, Kilmersdon, Radstock, Bath BA3 5SY

Robert Jackson and Co. Ltd, 172 Piccadilly, London W1
Also at 6a–6b Sloane Street, London SW1

C. Baldwin and Co., 173 Walworth Road, London SE17 1RW

Culpeper Ltd, 21 Bruton Street, London W1X 7DA
Also at 14 Bridwell Alley, Norwich, Norfolk
Mail order catalogue available from Culpeper Ltd, Hadstock Road, Cambridge

Chiltern Herb Farms Ltd, Buckland Common, Tring, Herts

The Bombay Emporium, 70 Grafton Way, London W1

Cranks, Marshall Street, London W1

John Bell and Croydon Ltd, Wigmore Street, London W1

In Australia

Melody Farm Nursery, 616 Old Northern Road, Dural, N.S.W. 2158

Hemphills Herbs and Spices Ltd, 745 Old Northern Road, Dural, N.S.W. 2158

Beaufort Herb Farm, P.O. Box 90, Cootamundra, N.S.W. 2590

Mitchell Lilydale Herb Farm, Mangans Road, Lilydale, Victoria 3140

Warrandyte Herbs, Huncy Road, Palmwoods, Qld 4555

Hygienic Products, 104 Bowden Street, West Ryde, N.S.W. 2114

Newton's Pharmacy, 323 Pitt Street, Sydney, N.S.W. 2000

Calorie Control Pty Ltd, 55 Benaroon Road, Belfield, N.S.W. 2191

Ralph Short Pty Ltd, 112 Durham Street, Hurstville, N.S.W. 2220

Triad Health Products Pty Ltd, P.O. Box 31, Asquith, N.S.W. 2078

Culpepers, 23Phillimore Street, Fremantle, W.A.

Lassocks Garden Centre, 334 Henley Beach Road, Locksleys, S.A.

In South Africa

Healthy Life, 10 Murchies Passage, West Street, Durban 400

Attwells Health Foods Ltd, 6 African Life Arcade, West Street, Durban 4001

Sunshine Health Centre, 84 Long Street, Cape Town 8001

Reform Health and Beauty, 287 Long Street, Cape Town 8001

Natural Remedies Centre and Health Food Shop, P.O. Box 5502, 2000 Johannesberg

F. Kirchoff and Co. Ltd, P.O. Box 7756, 2000 Johannesberg

Natural Medicinal Services Ltd, P.O. Box 4696, 2000 Johannesberg

Natural Homoeopathic Laboratory, 1221 Zanza Building, 16 Proes Street, 0002 Pretoria.

Index